DIGITAL ENTREPRENEURSHIP™
IN THE AGE OF APPS, THE WEB, AND MOBILE DEVICES

THE NEXT BIG THING

DEVELOPING YOUR DIGITAL BUSINESS IDEA

BARBARA GOTTFRIED HOLLANDER

ROSEN
PUBLISHING®

New York

For Ruthie, who is a computer whiz at a young age and always has great ideas

Published in 2013 by The Rosen Publishing Group, Inc.
29 East 21st Street, New York, NY 10010

First Edition

Library of Congress Cataloging-in-Publication Data

Hollander, Barbara, 1970–
The next big thing: developing your digital business idea/
Barbara Gottfried Hollander.—1st ed.
    p. cm.—(Digital entrepreneurship in the age of apps, the web, and mobile devices)
Includes bibliographical references and index.
ISBN 978-1-4488-6926-8 (library binding)
ISBN 978-1-4488-6931-2 (pbk.)—
ISBN 978-1-4488-6971-8 (6-pack)
1. Internet industry. 2. Electronic commerce.
3. Entrepreneurship. 4. New products. 5. New business enterprises. I. Title.
HD9696.8.A2H65 2013
004.068—dc23
                                                2012003029

Manufactured in the United States of America

CPSIA Compliance Information: Batch #S12YA: For further information, contact Rosen Publishing, New York, New York, at 1-800-237-9932.

CONTENTS

INTROD

At the end of 2011, Facebook's Mark Zuckerberg had an estimated net worth of $17.5 billion, according to *Forbes*. Jack Dorsey, cofounder and executive chairman of Twitter, had an estimated net worth of $650 million, and $300 million was the estimated net worth of YouTube's cofounder Chad Hurley. All of these rich young entrepreneurs earned their money by developing digital products.

Now, travel back in time to the 1980s and 1990s. It was a time of mass digitization, when many goods and services were launched into cyberspace. Digitization is the process of bringing products from the physical world into the virtual world, where they become digital. Digital products are goods and

UCTION

services that can be stored, used, and delivered in an electronic format. Today, they include a wide variety of products, including apps, Web sites, blogs, e-books, and the most popular, online social networks.

Owners of digital products do not pay manufacturing or distribution costs because digital products are downloaded from the Internet or shipped via e-mail. Although digital products are updated, these products can be made once and then sold many times. This provides large profit margins (amounts by which revenue, or income, exceeds costs) for digital

Above: Young technology leaders, including Twitter's Jack Dorsey, Bebo's Michael Birch, Skype's Niklas Zennström, YouTube's Chad Hurley, and Directi's Divyank Turakhia, met at an event called Founders in Dublin, Ireland, in 2010.

entrepreneurs. Entrepreneurs are people who create, organize, and run their own businesses.

Digital businesses use Internet technology, a combination of computing and telecommunications. This kind of technology transmits audio data (like a downloaded song), textual data (such as a blog or online tutorial), pictorial or visual data (like an online photo community), and numerical data. Digital entrepreneurs have a variety of mediums to choose from and often use combinations of different media. For example, a music video includes both audio and visual information. Technological advancements provide a growing number of opportunities for digital entrepreneurs.

CHAPTER 1

DEVELOP THE CONCEPT

Adigital business begins with an idea. As Kristopher Tate, creator of the Zooomr photo sharing community, told the magazine *.net*, "I'm just one person with an idea doing what I think is cool, and I'm glad to see that other people can partake in it."

Finding an interesting idea to share with others involves identifying one's interests and experiences. It also involves being aware of the needs that new products can fill. With some work, you can develop your ideas into successful digital products.

IDENTIFY YOUR INTERESTS AND EXPERIENCES

Developing a concept for a digital product requires brainstorming, or listing ideas. Begin with your areas of interest. Digital entrepreneurs who find their work interesting are more enthusiastic about it. Running a business is also time-consuming, so it helps to spend these hours doing something you find enjoyable. In an interview with Oliver Lindberg of *.net* magazine, teen entrepreneur Kristopher Tate said that when his company began, he was working nineteen hours each day.

Interests can be found in different places. Think about how you spend your free time. Review your

Teens interested in entertainment, fashion, and news can turn their passions into popular blogs. Teen blogger Tavi Gevinson covers fashion in her highly successful blog, Style Rookie.

favorite media, including your favorite television shows, movies, songs, books, and games. What school subjects, clubs, hobbies, and after-school activities have you enjoyed? Consider previous work experiences, volunteer work, and internships, too.

From an early age, Tate was interested in computers. At the age of four, he was working with HTML code, and by five, he had mastered the Mac. After his father bought a Macintosh Quadra 660AV, Tate developed apps for Macs, and he later began developing in the Windows environment. Tate also has an interest in photography. "I'm just some guy with a camera,"

Tate told Lindberg. "I try to document my life and, even before Zooomr, I tried to take at least one photo a day." Tate combined his interests in computers and photos to establish the online photo sharing community Zooomr.

When listing interests and experience, consult family, friends, and mentors. They may also have ideas for a product and help with your product's

Christian Owens founded Mac Bundle Box and an advertising pay-per-click company called Branchr. "I think everyone has business sense in them," Owens told the Daily Mail. "They just need to gain experience and be determined to make it."

development. For example, at the age of twelve, Freddie Anne Hodges had an app idea based on her interest in keeping track of her height. She shared it with her father. The result was an iPhone app called Measure Me that records body measurements. Also, consider the achievements of role models. Inspired by former Apple CEO Steve Jobs, sixteen-year-old Christian Owens made his first one million dollars in two years with his business Mac Bundle Box.

According to Rhonda Abrams, author of *What Business Should I Start?*, the most popular source for a business idea is work experience, while hobbies place second. However, beware: sometimes turning a hobby into work takes the fun out of it. For example, suppose that someone enjoys going to the movies, so she starts a movie review blog. At first, she enjoys attending lots of movies and writing reviews. But after a few months, she would rather spend her time doing other things. When turning a hobby into a digital business, be prepared to devote a great deal of time to the subject in a professional setting.

FILL A NEED

Digital business owners strive to provide products that others want to buy. This can be accomplished when those products fill a need. People have practical needs, such as using e-mail to communicate at work or a global positioning system (GPS) app to arrive at an unfamiliar destination. People also have psychological needs, such as interacting with friends on Facebook or being entertained by playing an online game. The goal

FINDING THE NEED

Young entrepreneur Mark Zuckerberg founded Facebook as a college sophomore. Zuckerberg was a Harvard student who identified the need for people to share information about themselves online and to stay in touch with family and friends. He also considered people's need to control information about themselves online at a time when information was becoming increasingly public and available. Zuckerberg was a forward thinker who spent time with friends talking about how the world was going to change in the future. Many of these friends shared his interests in computer science and psychology. Zuckerberg eventually developed an online social network. His original audience included about six thousand undergraduates at Harvard University, but it grew to include eight hundred million members across the world, as of fall 2011.

At the age of seven, Christian Owens had his first computer. By ten, he was doing Web design on a Mac, and by fourteen, Owens had founded a company called Mac Bundle Box. His company bundles together Mac OS X applications and sells them for discounted prices for a limited time. Owens identified a need for people to buy multiple apps at lower prices and negotiated with app developers to meet this need. For example, Mac Bundle Box may

According to the Nielsen Company, in 2010 gaming was the second most popular online activity, taking up 10 percent of Americans' time online (social networking was first, and e-mailing came in third). So, this digital entrepreneur decides to develop a new game with main characters that race around the world and encounter different adventures along the way. In order to travel to the next country—and level—players must use different currencies. The entrepreneur combined his interests and experience to develop a product that can fill a psychological need.

Reed Hastings cofounded an online DVD mail service called Netflix. Hastings then moved into streaming movies on televisions and computers, and the company continues to evolve.

Entrepreneurs are typically risk takers who are passionate about their visions. But, like everyone else, they are people with both strengths and weaknesses. When developing a digital business idea, entrepreneurs should assess their own attributes. For example, suppose a person's strengths include being organized, hardworking, and creative, while being outgoing is challenging. This entrepreneur could develop a product but might want to enlist help from others when contacting potential investors.

Developing a digital business idea is a process. It involves gaining awareness of one's interests, experiences, and personal attributes and other people's needs. Creating a successful digital product takes time and many attempts. As Catherine Cook said in an interview with JuniorBiz.com, "If your first idea doesn't work out, just try something new. Tweak the idea a little bit, and it could make a world of difference."

TURN IT AROUND

Like the founders of myYearbook, other digital entrepreneurs have turned challenges in their own lives into successful online business opportunities. Upset by a $40 video store late fee, Reed Hastings created an online DVD rental service with no late fees called Netflix. Cofounders Hastings and Marc Randolph revolutionized the movie rental market only a year after DVD players began selling in the United States. Within a month of Netflix's launch in 1998, the company had one thousand orders each day, which grew to over two thousand orders per day over the next three months. In 2011, Netflix was the largest online DVD rental company in the world, with over twenty million members.

David Lieb, cofounder and president of Bump Technologies, Inc., also turned an everyday problem into business success. "The idea for Bump came out of a moment of frustration (well, actually, two moments)," Lieb told Dave Wooldridge and Michael Schneider, authors of *The Business of iPhone and iPad App Development: Making and Marketing Apps*. "Back in 2005, I was working as an engineer, and it really bothered me that in order to get some simple data, like names and phone numbers from one phone to another one not 12 inches away from it, I had to ask someone to read out their information, and I had to type it in."

Lieb wanted to be able to just touch the phones together and transfer the information, but the phones of 2005 didn't have the technology needed to make that work. "Fast-forward to 2008, when I was in business school and found myself typing in the phone numbers of dozens of new classmates," Lieb continued. "Same frustration, but this time, I noticed everyone was carrying smartphones, many of which had accelerometers and location awareness. So we decided to build Bump." Bump is a free iPhone app that allows people to share information (like music, apps, messages, contacts, and calendar events) by bumping phones together. In 2010, Bump had over ten million downloads in Apple's App Store.

CHAPTER 2

DEFINE THE DIGITAL PRODUCT

After an entrepreneur identifies interests, experiences, and needs, he or she is ready to define the digital product. Digital products include online social forums, blogs, apps, and Web sites. Today, developers can launch apps on a variety of evolving platforms, providing many opportunities for digital entrepreneurs.

ONLINE SOCIAL FORUMS

Social networking refers to people coming together to form groups or communities. It fills both psychological and practical needs, including belonging, maintaining friendships, making new friends, sharing interests and information, developing professional contacts, and publicizing events. It is also the most popular way to spend time online. Top social networking sites include Facebook, Myspace, Twitter, and LinkedIn. Facebook is the largest social network, and LinkedIn is the largest professional network.

To develop an online social forum, find your niche, or specialized market. For example, the Cook siblings focused on digitizing a high school yearbook. Developing a social forum involves setting up a Web site and adding plug-ins that the target users will want. Plug-ins are additional pieces of software that increase the capabilities of the site. Popular plug-ins give users the ability to leave comments, play audio, download videos and songs, and bookmark favorites. To earn revenue, developers can charge their users directly. Or, they can provide their site free of charge to users and offer space to advertisers for a fee. Either way, social forum developers earn money by generating traffic. ("Traffic" refers to the number of users that visit a particular site.) The costs of developing an online social forum include building, maintaining, and updating the Web site, as well as doing marketing.

Social networking sites allow members to chat with friends, upload pictures and videos, share interests, organize events, reconnect with old friends, and make new ones—all at no financial cost and with round-the-clock accessibility.

BLOGS

A blog (short for "Web" and "log") is like a set of online journal entries, posted in reverse chronological order (with the most recent posts appearing first). Blogs are updated frequently and are often written informally. Bloggers can archive their older posts and add permalinks on their home pages for direct links to their most recent entries. Blogs document life events, provide news and information, or focus on an interest, such as movies, books, travel, fashion, or food. According to *Blogging for Dummies* by Susannah Gardner and Shane Birley, over 133 million blogs have been started since 2002. Technorati.com keeps track of over one million blogs, categorizing them by industry and ranking the most and least popular blogs.

Gardner and Birley recommend using the free service Blogger (http://www.blogger.com) to begin a blog. This site allows potential bloggers to create accounts, choose names, and select Web site templates. It also aids bloggers in posting entries, creating links, and publishing posts. An important feature for a blog is a comment section. Feedback provides inspiration for future posts, encourages a consistent customer base, and may result in updates to the site. Bloggers may also provide an e-mail address for readers to contact them directly.

As with online social forums, people who pursue blogging as a business typically aim to generate traffic and earn money through advertisements. Some blogs

Fashion blogger Jane Aldridge began a photo diary site in high school called Sea of Shoes. She has been able to influence consumers and even designers, launching a footwear collection in collaboration with Urban Outfitters.

have banner ads, while others have pop-up, blinking ads. Bloggers can also incorporate links that advertise goods and services. More users on a blog site increases earning potential because advertisers want to place ads where many people will see them. Aside from beginning a site, bloggers can also post on other people's sites for pay. For example, bloggers can join a network and search for paid blogging jobs on sites like PayPerPost.com. The sites ReviewMe.com, SponsoredReviews.com, and PayU2Blog.com also offer paid blogging opportunities.

Blogs fill both psychological needs (such as sharing life events) and practical ones (such as sharing information) for both bloggers and their users. Blogs can also lead to additional personal and professional opportunities. For example, professional blogger Beth Gottfried Lisogorsky wrote a weekly recap of episodes of the TV show *The Apprentice* (Season 1) for the Web site the Trades (http://www.the-trades.com). This led to coauthoring the book *10 Secrets I Learned from the Apprentice* with Anthony Parinello. Today, she has her own professional site, Amaldo.com, which she manages with her husband.

APPS (APPLICATIONS)

There are hundreds of thousands of apps on the market. There are apps that keep track of birthdays, provide gaming, build photo collages, create MTV-style videos, find new jobs, help with homework, and provide personal assistance while searching for a new home. Digital entrepreneurs define their app ideas with an outline, including the app name, purpose, a description of how the app looks and works, any needed graphics and audio, and how a person uses the app.

For example, take the popular iPhone app called *Bejeweled 2*. The purpose of this game is to make the most matches of three or more jewels, by swapping out other gems. More matches means higher scores. This puzzle game has a planetary backdrop with sparkly jewels in a boxed screen. There are also Score, Hint, Pause, and Menu buttons on the side of the

MAKING VIDEOS, BOOKS, AND MONEY

According to YouTube's company statistics, users upload more than forty-eight hours of video to the site every minute. YouTube, a subsidiary of Google, is a video-sharing Web site. It is also a way for digital entrepreneurs to earn money. YouTube has the revenue-sharing Partner Program, in which people upload videos and earn money from advertisements. YouTube estimates that over one-third of the most successful partners are under the age of twenty-five. For example, fifteen-year-old Megan Parker began a YouTube channel called Meganheartsmakeup that offers makeup tutorials and shopping advice. Within a short period of time, she had over one hundred thousand viewers per video and enough money to buy her own car. Megan earns money both from the Partner Program and from the companies whose brands she promotes.

Digital entrepreneurs can also create e-products, such as e-books. E-books are fiction or nonfiction books that are published and accessed online. People can self-publish e-books, at a cost. As with all products, pricing is important. Many successful e-books are priced at less than $5. Authors should choose agreements that enable them to determine their own prices. Popular self-publishing sites for e-books include Amazon's DTP, Barnes & Noble

PubIt, Smashwords, Lulu, Scribd, and FastPencil. A digital author earns money from a royalty, or a percentage of the book's retail price. Royalties depend on the publisher and the location of the sale. For example, Smashwords pays authors 60 percent royalties on e-books sold through the Apple iBookstore, but only 42.5 percent on the same e-books sold through the Barnes & Noble e-bookstore.

boxed area. As users make matches, points appear among the jewels. There are three game modes, with landscape and portrait displays, and the game has special effects. A user downloads the game to the iPhone and uses a touch screen to play.

Some entrepreneurs both define and develop ideas for apps. For these entrepreneurs, Apple provides a setting for creating and testing apps. By 2010, Apple had 50 percent of the mobile gaming market. Its iPod touch outsold all of Nintendo's and Sony's mobile products put together. Other entrepreneurs define their apps and then hire third parties to develop them. In the case of Measure Me, twelve-year-old Freddie Anne Hodges defined her app idea but paid an independent developer to build the app. Successful apps are easy to use, visually appealing, affordable, and well marketed (so spread the word about your app!).

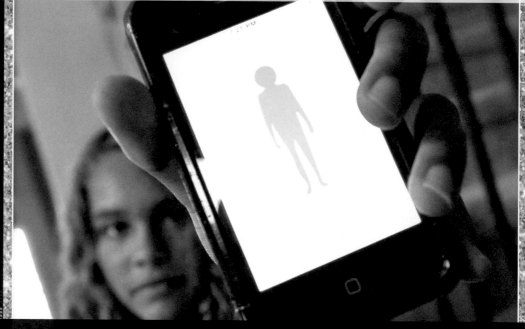

 At the age of twelve, Freddie Anne Hodges developed the idea for an app called Measure Me. It uses the iPhone's camera function to track body measurements.

DEFINING YOUR NICHE

A niche is a particular area of demand within the market that entrepreneurs target. For example, the site Candyblog (http://www.candyblog.com) focuses just on candy. Finding a niche is one of the first steps in defining a product because it answers the question, "What does my product offer that existing products do not?" If an entrepreneur develops a completely original product, he or she already has a niche, since the new product is automatically different from others in the market. At other times, defining a niche involves finding a new twist on an existing product or targeting a new

People can view blogs on digital devices, such as computers, cell phones, and iPads. Pets are one of the most popular blogging niches. Blog posts often include pictures with captions.

demographic, such as teens. In her book *Nichecraft: Using Your Specialness to Focus Your Business, Corner Your Market, and Make Customers Seek You Out*, Lynda Falkenstein gives seven steps for creating your own niche, including targeting a specific market and viewing the market from the customer's perspective. When developing a niche, consider if customers will think your product offers something new.

CHAPTER 3

EVALUATE THE MARKET

D eveloping an idea and defining a product are the first two steps in beginning a digital business. Once a product is defined, digital entrepreneurs assess the market for their goods. A market is where buyers and sellers meet to exchange goods and services for money or barter. Within the market, there may be competition, or other sellers who offer similar digital products for sale. Part of developing a digital business is evaluating the business's potential customers, competition, and risks.

FIND THE IDEAL CUSTOMER

An important step in beginning a business is defining the market. Begin with the ideal customers. Are they consumers? This means your business follows the "business to consumer," or B2C, model. Or are they other businesses? This is known as the "business to business," or B2B, model. For example, if a business, such as Apple's iTunes, is selling music, then the customers are consumers. But, if a business provides teleseminars or online courses to help train employees, then businesses may be the customers.

For Mark Zuckerberg of Facebook, his original target audience was the group of more than six thousand

Integrating the touch and tilt features of the iPhone, avid gamer Steve Demeter created a puzzle game called Trism. It was the first "match three" game that included the iPhone's tilting component.

students at his college, Harvard University. For Catherine and David Cook of myYearbook, their original target audience was the student body at their high school, Montgomery High School in Skillman, New Jersey. So, do these online social networking sites follow the B2C model? No, because the audiences for Facebook and myYearbook are not their customers. A customer is someone who pays for a good or service. Like television shows, these online forums earn money from companies that pay to advertise their goods and services on the sites. Advertisers are actually

Facebook and myYearbook's customers. The more users that these sites have, the greater the demand is to advertise on them. These social networking sites are examples of the B2B model because their customers are businesses.

The model for some app developers is B2C. These developers are targeting consumers, who will pay to download their digital products. For example, consider someone who develops an iPhone app. The entrepreneur sells the product through the iPhone App Store, which keeps 30 percent of the revenue and gives 70 percent to the developer. The individuals who download the app, usually for a price between $0.99 and $9.99, are the customers. Using the B2C model, iPhone developer Steve Demeter earned $250,000 in two months from his game, *Trism*. Ethan Nicholas topped that figure with the $600,000 that he earned from selling the iPhone game *iShoot*.

After identifying the ideal customer, envision the driving forces behind this customer's choices. Is it price? Will customers' buying habits change a lot if the price changes (known in economics as "elasticity")? Does the customer respond to peer influence, such as joining a particular online social forum or playing a certain online game because his or her friends are doing it? (Consider friends, family, and work contacts when thinking about people that may influence others.) Are your customers motivated by convenience? In that case, they may be attracted to apps that link a lot of information together. Do customers respond to the delivery method, such as being accessible from an iPhone?

APP DEVELOPMENT PLATFORMS:
APPLE AND ANDROID

On June 23, 2010, the Android cell phones launched. The iPhone 4 was released the next day. That year, Google also introduced a platform for developers, Google App Inventor, for Android apps. This created more opportunities for app developers and more competition for Apple. Both Apple and Google strive to make app development accessible to all, but there are some differences between them:

- Apple apps run on iPhones. Android apps run on Android phones, such as those made by Motorola, Sony, and LG. In 2010, Apple supported paid apps in ninety countries, while Android supported paid apps in only thirty-two countries.

- Apple has an approval process for new apps (with a very high acceptance rate), while Google asks developers only to complete its form. As a result, it takes an average of four days for Apple to accept a new app, but only ten seconds for an Android app to become available for sale in the Android market.

- Apple app developers earn more money than Android app developers. According to a 2011 *USA TODAY* article by Byron Acohido, piracy (illegal downloading, copying, and republish-ing) is partly to blame. The Yankee Group research firm found that 27 percent of Android developers believe piracy is a huge problem. More than a third said that piracy has cost them more than $10,000 in revenue.

After answering these questions, make a profile of the ideal customer and user. Include demographics, such as age, gender, occupation, geographical location, buying habits, and income levels. Awareness of the buying habits and preferences of customers helps to anticipate long-run growth. Look for ways of targeting the most profitable customer base. For example, you may seek to generate more Web traffic to increase the demand for advertising space. Also, keep in mind the type of person that you are *not* selling to; remem-ber that you cannot be everything to everyone.

RESEARCH THE COMPETITION

Some digital entrepreneurs, like Steve Jobs and Netflix's Reed Hastings and Marc Randolph, revolution-ized industries with new inventions. But, many entrepreneurs do not reinvent the wheel; they take existing products and add their own twists. These entrepreneurs hope that their changes will distinguish them from their competition, or other producers who supply similar products. When developing, designing, and marketing a new product, figure out what makes your product different from the competition.

Developing a digital business idea takes research. Working with others can add experience, financial resources, and contacts to your team.

For example, when Kristopher Tate founded Zooomr, another photo sharing community site called Flickr already existed. Like Flickr, Zooomr offers both a paid service and a free version with limited bandwidth (paid for by advertisers). Both photo sharing sites also allow members to view photos in squares, thumbnails, and different sizes. So what makes Zooomr different from the competition? Zooomr is less expensive, at $20 per year, but it's Zooomr's focus that sets it apart from the rest.

"I like Yahoo! and Flickr; I think they are great people," Tate told blogger Thomas Hawk. "What Zooomr tries to accomplish is not organizing like Flickr does so well, but actually getting at the metadata that a photo represents." For example, Zooomr combines recorded audio with photos to tell the story behind an image, something that Tate calls a "Zooomrtation." Tate also introduced geotagging—adding geographical identification—months before Yahoo!'s photo site.

Find out about competitors by visiting their sites or researching their products (gaming counts!). How are they doing in the marketplace? Are competitors selling many products and earning profits? What is their niche? Some businesses may sell the same product but position themselves differently, like Zooomr and Flickr do. Another photo site called Clipart.com has yet another angle. Rather than dealing with personal pic-tures, the site allows subscribers to download others' photos and artwork for creative projects. Find your "unique selling advantage" or "unique selling proposi-tion" that sets you apart from your competitors. Is it price, quality, focus, a new product, or another factor?

HIDDEN COSTS

There are opportunity costs to developing and selling digital products. These costs include ways you could have spent resources (such as time and money) other than running a digital business. Young entrepreneurs are often in school and are still responsible for their academics, social commitments, and other extracurricular activities. Developing and running a digital business takes time away from studying, hanging out with friends, earning revenues in other ways, and sleeping. According to an interview with Catherine Cook on JuniorBiz.com, during her first year of college, Cook's best friend and roommate discovered how much time she devoted to myYearbook and said, "You never sleep!" Likewise, the money an entrepreneur spends developing and selling a digital product could be spent on other things, such as movies, electronics, clothes, and charity.

MARKET RESEARCH

Digital entrepreneurs can use search engines such as Google and Yahoo! to find out about businesses that offer similar products. They can also examine data from market research companies, trade associations, and small business organizations. Find out what works

At the age of fourteen, Ashley Qualls launched a content resource Web site and online community called WhateverLife .com. Her popular site offers Web graphics and layouts, such as Myspace layouts and iPhone wallpapers.

for the competition, such as offering free membership. Gaining knowledge about the market does not neces-sarily mean following what everyone else does. It means making an informed decision about what to follow and what to do differently.

Learn about what challenges the competition has faced. For example, both Facebook and Netflix took off even faster than anticipated, which created difficulties at times. According to *The Complete Idiot's Guide to Business Plans*, budding entrepreneurs should also examine whether more people are using a certain type of product more often (like social networking, online gaming, and streaming videos and movies in 2010) or less frequently (such as instant messaging in 2010). Keep informed about technological advancements and industry changes. For example, the introductions of the iPhone, iPad, and iOS made it possible for almost anyone to develop apps.

KNOW YOUR RISKS

Beginning a business is a risky venture. Larger businesses often carry greater risks because people invest more time and money into their operations. Some entrepreneurs begin with large businesses, while others expand their businesses as their member and customer bases grow. Sometimes, entrepreneurs take out loans, or borrow money, from banks and other financial institutions. Entrepreneurs need to pay start-up costs, such as domain name registration or accessing a development kit, even if their products never sell. Losing money is a risk in starting a digital business, or any business.

But, the digital medium most likely reduces some of these financial risks. According to an article by Darren Dahl on AOL Small Business, online companies are ideal for teens because of their low start-up costs. In fact, Dahl mentions that an online business, like starting a blog, can be established for less than $50. In 2004, at the age of fourteen, Ashley Qualls started an online company called WhateverLife by borrowing $8 from her mother to pay for the domain name. Her site offers free Myspace layouts and both graphic design and coding tutorials. By 2011, she had seven million visits to her site a month, and she received an offer of $1.5 million to purchase her site.

MYTHS & FACTS

MYTH: All digital business ideas are original.

FACT: Many digital business ideas tweak existing products.

MYTH: Market research is not important until the product is already developed.

FACT: Market research is done throughout the business planning and development process. It enables entrepreneurs to find their niche, target ideal customers, learn about the competition, and assess risk.

MYTH: Digital product users are always the customers.

FACT: Digital product users are sometimes the customers. For example, many online forums are free for users and paid for by advertisers. In those cases, the advertisers are the customers.

CHAPTER 4

WRITE A BUSINESS PLAN

A business plan is a road map for both the entrepreneur and others involved in the business. It defines goals and how the business will attempt to meet them. A business plan communicates the direction of the company to others and provides documentation needed for financial support. This plan also defines a business's vision, keeps a company focused, and supports its expansion.

MAKE A STATEMENT

According to *The Complete Idiot's Guide to Business Plans*, a business plan has up to three statements. The mission statement describes what a company is offering. For example, Facebook's site describes its mission as "Giving people the power to share and make the world more open and connected." A mission statement can also include reasons for beginning a company and a description of its niche. The vision statement shares the company's long-term goals (goals for five to ten years in the future), such as expanding an audience base from several schools to hundreds of schools. Finally, the value statement conveys the company's priorities, such as providing an affordable app at a low price and earning higher profits each year.

Writing a business plan puts your ideas, future plans, and resources on paper. It allows you to share this information with your team and potential investors.

Statements are updated as companies grow. For example, Apple Inc.'s 2009 press releases included a statement that described the past, present, and future accomplishments of the company. Among its future goals were "spearhead[ing] the digital media revolution" and becoming more involved in the mobile phone market. In 2011, Apple updated this statement to include being the leader in the digital music revolution, reinventing the mobile phone, and introducing the iPad 2, which the company said is "defining the future of mobile media and computing devices."

COMPONENTS OF A BUSINESS PLAN

A business plan is a written report. Like a research paper, it has a title page with the company's name, address, phone and fax numbers, e-mail and Web site addresses, owners' names, and trademark (if applicable). A cover letter appears right before the title page and table of contents. The cover letter includes the company's name, address, contact information, and date. It states a goal, such as obtaining a specified amount of start-up funding. It also suggests the next steps, such as setting up a call or meeting, and mentions enclosed materials, including the business plan and any additional financial documents.

The first main section is the executive summary. This summary is an entrepreneur's chance to prove the company's worth. It's like an introduction to a book. If others find the summary interesting, they will read more. An executive summary is a shortened version of the business plan, which explains why others, such as investors, would want to join the company. The mission, vision, and value statements are usually part of the executive summary, too.

The rest of the business plan includes sections that provide more details.

- The company section discusses the business's history and owners.
- The product and services section fully describes the product, its competitive edge, and even future business products like updates to an app.

- The organization and management section discusses how the company is organized and its legal structure.

- The market analysis section includes market research results, such as market trends and growth (like the increasing popularity of gaming). It also describes the business's specific target market and main competitors.

- The financial section covers information such as expected revenues, profits, and losses. This part also discloses the break-even analysis, or the product quantity that needs to be sold at a particular price in order to cover costs.

Business plans can also include separate sections on strategies for pricing, marketing (such as Web advertising), and sales.

REASONS FOR A PLAN

Entrepreneurs develop business plans for different reasons, including beginning, expanding, or selling a business. Companies share their business plans with potential investors to obtain needed funding. If investors choose to be a part of a business, they can provide loans (known as debt financing) or become part owners in the business (known as equity financing). Both forms of financing provide money for business owners, but debt financing means repaying the loans, while equity financing means a greater number of people running the business. The business

Business Plan Templates and Software

Online business templates provide preformatted plans and examples that make writing a business plan easier. The U.S. Small Business Administration (SBA) generates a business plan at no charge after completion of online fill-in-the-blank forms (http://web.sba.gov/busplantemplate/BizPlanStart.cfm). SCORE, a nonprofit association that helps entrepreneurs, is another provider of free business plan templates for start-ups and established companies. See its gallery of templates at http://www.score.org/resources/business-plans-financial-statements-template-gallery. The organization offers e-mail mentors to answer questions, too.

There are also business plan software packages that generally cost $100 or more. For example, Bplans (http://www.bplans.com) sells business plan software. It also provides free samples of business plans, organized by industry. Business Plan Pro Premier from Palo Alto Software (http://www.paloalto.com/business_plan_software/features/premier#) is another business plan software product. It includes over five hundred sample plans, market comparison tools, and financial spreadsheets to help forecast expenses, sales, and growth.

plan also outlines resource allocation, or how resources (like money, workers, and equipment) will be used to begin or expand the company. Finally, a business plan can provide information to investors who are willing to buy the whole company. Many investors are eager to purchase successful digital companies. For example, the Latino social network Quepasa Corporation bought myYearbook for $100 million in 2011.

Investors are particularly interested in the financial section of a business plan. Information on revenues and profits are found in this section. Revenue is the money earned from selling goods and services. Profit is any money left over from revenues, after the business's expenses are paid. People invest in a company because they hope to earn more money from their investments in the future. Profits are an indicator of

U.S. Small Business Administration

SBA

Your Small Business Resource

Business Plan Template

| Template Home - Start |
| Executive Summary |
| Business Description and Vision |
| Definition of the Market |
| Description of the Products and Services |
| Organization and Management |
| Marketing and Sales Strategy |

Business Description and Vision

This section should include:

- Mission statement (business purpose).
- Company vision (statement about company growth).
- Business goals and objectives.
- Brief history of the business.
- List of key company principals.

After reviewing this section the reader should know:

- Who the business is and what it stands for.
- Your perception of the company's growth & potential.
- Specific goals and objectives of the business.
- Background information about the company.

The U.S. Small Business Administration (SBA) provides templates that generate business plans. The SBA also offers information and training, including podcasts, on starting, managing, and financing a business.

the rate of return on an investment. Effectively outlining a company's profit-earning potential can be challenging, especially for start-up companies that do not have established track records.

A business plan can also be used as an internal management tool. By distributing the plan within the company, employees know benchmarks, short-term goals, and long-term goals. A benchmark is a standard for comparison used to measure goal attainment. For example, suppose a business plan is a road map with the goal of traveling from Washington to Boston. A possible benchmark would be Philadelphia because it is a place along the route. By meeting benchmarks, a company is more likely to meet its goals. Updating business plans allows employees to redirect as needed, such as changing an advertising project to target different customers.

Sharing business plans within the company encourages managers to work toward the same goals.

10 GREAT QUESTIONS TO ASK A FINANCIAL ADVISER

1 How much money do I need to develop a digital product?

2 Are certain digital products less expensive to develop than others?

3 How do I determine a price for my digital product?

4 How do I figure out how much money I will earn from each sale (my revenue)?

5 How do I calculate my business's profit?

6 Do I pay taxes on my company's earnings?

7 What should I include in the financial section of my business plan?

8 What financial documents should accompany my business plan?

9 Who are the best investors for my company?

10 What are the advantages of debt versus equity financing?

CHAPTER 5

CHOOSING A BUSINESS STRUCTURE AND PROTECTING INTELLECTUAL PROPERTY RIGHTS

D igital business entrepreneurs can choose from different business structures. They also have options for protecting their intellectual property, or creative achievements used in business. The U.S. government protects intellectual property rights to encourage people to invent new products. This protection allows people to earn money from their products and prevents others from taking their ideas.

BUSINESS OWNERSHIP

There are different business structures, or ways of legally establishing your business, including a sole proprietorship, a partnership, and a corporation. A sole proprietorship refers to a business owned by one person, while a partnership is a business owned by two or more people. These business structures have several advantages over a corporation. For example, the owners are in charge of all decisions, there is minimal paperwork, and there are some tax benefits. Sole proprietorships and partnerships also have disadvantages. For example, any debts are the owner's responsibility. If a business fails, the owner personally has to repay any money owed. Sole proprietorships and partnerships may also have more difficulty in borrowing the money needed for financing.

In 2010, Time magazine named Facebook CEO and cofounder Mark Zuckerberg its "Person of the Year." In 2012, Facebook still ranked as the most popular social networking site and was expected to reach one billion users that year.

Many successful young digital entrepreneurs have chosen to begin corporations. Some incorporated themselves later as their companies grew. "It occurred to me that building a company was the best way to align a group of people towards building something great...It's a good organizational structure where you can really reward people," Facebook founder Mark Zuckerberg told BusinessInsider.com. Another example of a teen starting a corporation is Zooomr. In 2006, at the age of seventeen, Kristopher Tate founded online photo sharing company Zooomr Inc. He remains its chief technologist. Tate also founded two other product design and innovation companies, BlueBridge Technologies and AM6.jp, both located in Japan.

A corporation is a legal entity. It owns assets (valuable items) and liabilities (debts). Corporations have many advantages, including limited liability. This means that if a business fails, the company (not the owner personally) is responsible for all money owed. Another advantage includes receiving tax benefits and deductions, such as writing off a business trip. Corporations are also more likely to receive needed funds from investors. For example, within six years, the social networking site myYearbook was able to raise $17 million in financing. Disadvantages of a corporation include higher start-up costs, including fees required by individual states and possible lawyer fees. Corporations also entail more paperwork, such as financial statements and payroll records for employees.

Some teens view their age as an advantage to beginning a company. For example, in 2005, teen siblings Catherine and Dave Cook founded Insider Guides Inc., to run myYearbook. "One of the main advantages was that there was no risk to starting a company—I was still in high school and living at my mom's house," Catherine Cook told SocialTimes.com. "The worst thing that could happen was that we couldn't get anyone to join and that we would fail, but then we'd still have a pretty cool college application essay to write anyway."

APPLICATION CONTENT PROVIDER AGREEMENTS

Digital entrepreneurs may also choose to be third party, independent application content providers (ACPs) with existing network companies. ACPs develop applications and services, such as mobile and multiscreen videos, mobile gaming, and visual memorization. Then they enter into agreements with network providers, who provide access, bandwidth (frequency range to transmit signals), and packet management (such as installation and upgrading). These agreements specify the terms, such as ownership of content and payment method.

According to Karl Bream, author of *Increasing Network Relevancy With Advanced Business Models*, there are different models to consider. In one model, the end user of the content pays a network service provider for it. The ACP provides content to the provider, who distributes content and serves as the contact for subscribers. For example, Apple provides songs to Belgacom iTunes portal. In return, Belgacom pays Apple a percentage of downloads and sales commissions, and Apple pays the content owner.

In another model, the ACP pays the network provider for delivering content and applications, and the end user pays the ACP to buy these services. Bream cites Amazon's use of the Sprint network for Kindle e-books as an example of this model.

DOMAIN REGISTRATION

Online businesses require domain names, or Web addresses. When selecting a domain name, choose one that is easy to remember and describes the product. Some Web sites provide name suggestions and reveal availability. For instance, suppose that a person wants to start a movie blog site. She types in movie blog on Panabee (http://www.panabee.com), which discloses that movieblog.com is unavailable as a domain name. This site also suggests alternatives, like movieblg.com, getmovieblog.com, and movieblogisto.com. Bust a Name (http://www.bustaname.com) is another site that provides domain name suggestions.

After ensuring that a domain name is unique, the next step is registration. The Federal Trade Commission (FTC) warns of registration scams, like preregistration services that guarantee top-level domain names (such as .gov, .info., or .name). The InterNIC Web site (http://www.internic.net) provides a list of legitimate registrars. The InterNIC site is run by the Internet Corporation for Assigned Names and Numbers (ICANN), which ensures unique domain names and valid, locatable addresses. There are over fifteen thousand ".com" registrations every week!

The third model involves brokers that pay network providers. According to Bream, "This model is for situations where multiple ACPs provide content, such as video, to a content aggregator, who in turn funnels it to the Internet through a single portal owned by a content delivery network (CDN) operator."

Application content providers can develop their content for a digital application and then contact a company that provides distribution channels. For example, an entrepreneur develops a book and wants to distribute it through iBookstore using iTunes Connect. The e-book author can fill out an application at the Apple Web site to partner with Apple as a content provider. Digital content providers can also submit music, television, and movie content by completing an iTunes Connect online application.

Now, suppose that a digital entrepreneur makes a new iPhone app and wants to sell it through the Apple App Store. First, the entrepreneur downloads and installs the SDK and Xcode development system through the iOS Developer Program. There is a cost of $99 per year to access the tools, once installed. The next steps involve running the keychain access app, receiving a certificate signing request, and registering the entrepreneur's iPhone as a testing device. According to Apple, the company receives 8,500 apps per week and accepts 95 percent of submissions within the first two weeks.

Countries that download the most free apps are the United States, China, Japan, South Korea, the UK, Germany, France, and Canada. Weekends are the busiest time to download.

PROTECTING INTELLECTUAL PROPERTY

The U.S. government uses different kinds of legally enforceable tools to protect intellectual property. For example, patents can protect Internet tools (such as search engines or e-commerce systems) and some software. A patent allows the inventor to be the only person who can produce, use, and sell an invention for up to twenty years. The Patent Cooperation Treaty addresses international patent

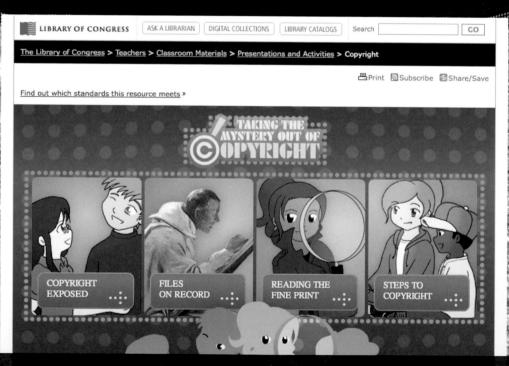

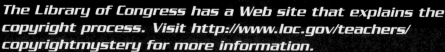

The Library of Congress has a Web site that explains the copyright process. Visit http://www.loc.gov/teachers/copyrightmystery for more information.

protection. The U.S. Patent and Trademark Office handles patent protection within the United States. An inventor or a patent lawyer can apply for a patent. However, using a patent lawyer can cost thousands of dollars.

For a less expensive alternative, inventors can file an online application, using EFS-web. Application fees vary, but as of September 2011, the basic fee for filing a utility patent application was $380. There are three kinds of patents, including utility, design, and plant. Business method patents, also known as Internet patents, are considered utility patents because they protect a process rather than a tangible good. Patent applicants receive electronic receipts and confirmation, after forms are complete.

A copyright is another way to protect intellectual property, including Web site design, creative content (such as written material, music, videos, and photographs), some software, and databases. While patents protect inventions or discoveries, copyrights cover authored works. Registration requires a nonrefundable fee of $35 and copies of the protected work. Inventors must complete the appropriate copyright form, which can be submitted electronically or mailed. Registering a work with the U.S. Copyright Office, a division of the Library of Congress, allows for legal protection and the right to sue for infringements (violations).

Like a copyright, a trademark is established through use but receives legal protection from an accepted registration through a federal agency. A trademark consists of words, phrases, symbols, or designs that identify a particular good or service, like app icons. The symbol of an "R" inside a circle is the federal registration symbol that applies to trademarks registered with the U.S. Patent and Trademark Office. Entrepreneurs can complete and submit their applications online, using the Trademark Electronic Application System (TEAS). Application fees are nonrefundable and range from $275 to $375. This process can be more expensive if using an attorney.

Take the time to protect your digital product. It is your personal creation that meets needs and generates revenue. Use your interests, experiences, and contacts to develop your digital business idea and fulfill your dreams. As myYearbook's Catherine Cook said on JuniorBiz.com, "Go for your goals. Don't let anyone tell you that you can't do it."

GLOSSARY

APPLICATION (APP) Computer software that allows a user to perform a function or functions.

BLOG Online journal entries, such as commentaries or descriptive narratives, usually placed in reverse-chronological order.

BUSINESS PLAN A statement of business goals and ways to achieve them.

COMPETITION Sellers competing for the same customers or market.

CONTENT PROVIDER A person who stores data, retrieves data, and provides access to apps.

COPYRIGHT A right granted to the author of an original work to be the only one who can reproduce, publish, sell, or distribute the work.

DIGITAL PRODUCTS Goods or services that can be stored, used, and delivered in an electronic format.

DOMAIN NAME Web address.

ENTREPRENEUR A person who organizes and runs his or her own business.

INTELLECTUAL PROPERTY Property, such as an idea, invention, or process, that comes from the work of the mind.

MARKET A place where buyers and sellers exchange goods and services for money or barter.

MISSION STATEMENT A description of what a company offers.

NICHE The particular area of demand for a product.

PATENT A government grant that allows a person to produce, use, and sell an invention for up to twenty years.

SOCIAL NETWORKING SITE A Web site that facilitates people coming together to form online groups or communities.

TRADEMARK Words, phrases, symbols, or designs that identify a particular good or service.

Canadian Youth Business Foundation (CYBF)

100 Adelaide Street West, Suite 1410
Toronto, ON M5H 1S3
Canada
(866) 646-2922
Web site: http://www.cybf.ca

The Canadian Youth Business Foundation provides professional advice, business resources, and financial support for entrepreneurs, ages eighteen to thirty-four. The foundation helps young businesspeople from the initial concept and planning to implementation, growth, and measurement. Financial assistance is made possible with the assistance of the Business Development Bank of Canada.

Internet Corporation for Assigned Names and Numbers (ICANN)

4676 Admiralty Way, Suite 330
Marina del Rey, CA 90292-6601
(310) 823-9358
Web site: http://www.icann.org

This internationally organized, nonprofit corporation is responsible for Internet Protocol (IP). It provides information on domain registration, legitimate registrars, and domain disputes.

Junior Achievement of Canada

1 Eva Road
Etobicoke, ON M9C 4Z5
Canada
(416) 622-4602
Web site: http://www.jacan.org

Junior Achievement is a nonprofit organization dedicated to inspiring and preparing youth to succeed in a global economy. Its programs, which include innovative business simulations, enable young people to develop essential life skills. Junior Achievement reaches over 250,000 students annually with 15,000 dedicated business volunteers in more than 400 communities across Canada.

Junior Achievement USA
One Education Way
Colorado Springs, CO 80906
(719) 540-8000
Web site http://www.ja.org
Junior Achievement is the world's largest organization that teaches entrepreneurship, financial literacy, and work readiness. The organization impacts four million U.S. students in more than 173,000 classrooms. Its site provides information on Junior Achievement offices throughout the country.

Youth Business America
469 9th Street, Suite 240
Oakland, CA 94607-4041
(510) 444-5511
Web site: http://www.youthbusinessamerica.org
Youth Business America supports young entrepreneurs who want to begin their own businesses. It provides one-on-one volunteer business mentoring and loan assistance to entrepreneurs who meet requirements.

WEB SITES

Due to the changing nature of Internet links, Rosen Publishing has developed an online list of Web sites related to the subject of this book. This site is updated regularly. Please use this link to access the list:

http://www.rosenlinks.com/deaa/nbt

FOR FURTHER READING

Abrams, Rhonda M. *Successful Business Plan: Secrets and Strategies*. 5th ed. Palo Alto, CA: The Planning Shop, 2010.

Conder, Shane, and Lauren Darcey. *Android Wireless Application Development* (Developer's Library). Upper Saddle River, NJ: Addison-Wesley, 2010.

Feiler, Jesse. *Get Rich with Apps! Your Guide to Reaching More Customers and Making Money Now*. New York, NY: McGraw-Hill, 2010.

Hansen, Mark Victor. *The Richest Kids in America: How They Earn It, How They Spend It, How You Can Too*. Newport Beach, CA: Hansen House, 2009.

Howard, Tharon. *Design to Thrive: Creating Social Networks and Online Communities That Last*. San Francisco, CA: Morgan Kaufmann Publishers, Inc., 2010.

Hussey, Tris. *Create Your Own Blog: 6 Easy Projects to Start Blogging Like a Pro*. Upper Saddle River, NJ: Pearson Education, Inc., 2010.

Lewis, Rory. *iPhone and iPad Apps for Absolute Beginners*. New York, NY: Apress, 2010.

Mureta, Chad. *Make Millions with Apps: Simple Steps to Turn Your App Idea into Profit*. Hoboken, NJ: Wiley, 2012.

Rankin, Kenrya, Eriko Takada, and Melissa Fiend. *Start It Up: The Complete Teen Business Guide for Turning Your Passions into Pay*. San Francisco, CA: Zest Books, 2011.

Rich, Jason, and J. S. McDougall. *Start Your Own Blogging Business*. 2nd ed. Irvine, CA: J. L. Calmes, 2010.

Stevens, Chris. *Appillionaires: Secrets from Developers Who Struck It Rich on the App Store*. Oxford, England: Wiley, 2011.

Stim, Richard. *Patent, Copyright & Trademark: An Intellectual Property Desk Reference*. Berkley, CA: Nolo Press, 2010.

Topp, Carol. *Starting a Micro Business*. Cincinnati, OH: Ambassador Publishing, 2010.

Yarmosh, Ken. *App Savvy: Turning Ideas into iPad and iPhone Apps Customers Really Want*. Farnham, England: O'Reilly, 2011.

Abrams, Rhonda M. *What Business Should I Start?* Palo Alto, CA: Planning Shop, 2004.

Acohido, Byron. "Android Apps Less Profitable Than iPhone Apps." *USA Today*, September 8, 2011. Retrieved November 2011 (http://content.usatoday.com/communities/technologylive/post/2011/09/android-apps-less-profitable-than-iphone-apps/1).

Apple.com. "Apple Developer Programs—Apple Developer." Retrieved October 2011 (http://developer.apple.com/programs).

Apple.com. "Apple—Press Info—Apple Names Arthur D. Levinson Chairman of the Board." November 15, 2011. Retrieved November 2011 (http://www.apple.com/pr/library/2011/11/15en-US-Apple-Names-Arthur-D-Levinson-Chairman-of-the-Board.html).

Apple.com. "Apple—Press Info—Apple to Ship Mac OS X Snow Leopard on August 28." August 24, 2009. Retrieved October 2011 (http://www.apple.com/pr/library/2009/08/24Apple-to-Ship-Mac-OS-X-Snow-Leopard-on-August-28.html).

Arden, Lynie, and Robert McGarvey. *Start Your Own e-Business*. 2nd ed. Irvine, CA: Jere L. Calmes, 2009.

Barnatt, Christopher. "The Second Digital Revolution." ExplainingTheFuture.com, July 2, 2011. Retrieved October 2011 (http://www.explainingthefuture.com/sdr.html).

Blodget, Henry. "Mark Zuckerberg, Moving Fast and Breaking Things." BusinessInsider.com, October 14, 2010. Retrieved November 2011 (http://www.businessinsider.com/mark-zuckerberg-2010-10#ixzz1eDAb2yS8).

Bolton, David. "How Do I Sell My iPhone App Via the App Store?" About.com. Retrieved November 2011 (http://cplus.about.com/od/iphonecodingtutorials/a/app_store_development.htm).

Bream, Karl. *Increasing Network Relevancy with Advanced Business Models*. Alcatel-Lucent, 2009. Retrieved November 2011 (http://www.tmcnet.com/redir/?u=1003482).

Carnoy, David. "How to Self-Publish an E-book." CNET, November 9, 2010. Retrieved November 2011 (http://reviews.cnet.com/how-to-self-publish-an-e-book).

Chen, Brian X. "Coder's Half-Million-Dollar Baby Proves iPhone Gold Rush Is Still On." Wired.com, February 12, 2009. Retrieved November 2011 (http://www.wired.com/gadgetlab/2009/02/shoot-is-iphone).

Dahl, Darren. "The Best Business Ideas for Teens." AOL Small Business, May 10, 2010. Retrieved October 2011 (http://smallbusiness.aol.com/2010/05/10/the-best-business-ideas-for-teens).

Diaz, Jesus. "How a 16-yo Kid Made His First Million Dollars Following His Hero, Steve Jobs." Gizmodo.com, August 13, 2010. Retrieved November 2011 (http://gizmodo.com/5612145/how-a-16+yo-kid-made-his-first-million-dollars-following-his-hero-steve-jobs).

Falkenstein, Lynda. *Nichecraft: Using Your Specialness to Focus Your Business, Corner Your Market, and Make Customers Seek You Out*. 2nd ed. Portland, OR: NichePress, 2000.

Forbes. "Mark Zuckerberg." November 2011. Retrieved November 15, 2011 (http://www.forbes.com/profile/mark-zuckerberg).

Gardner, Susannah, and Shane Birley. *Blogging for Dummies*. 3rd ed. Hoboken, NJ: Wiley, 2010.

Good, Owen. "Gaming Surpasses E-mail in Time Spent Online." Kotaku.com, August 4, 2010. Retrieved November 2011 (http://kotaku.com/5604793/gaming-surpasses-email-in-time-spent-online).

Hawgood, Alex. "No Stardom Until After Homework." *New York Times*, July 15, 2011. Retrieved November 2011 (http://www.nytimes.com/2011/07/17/fashion/how-teenagers-handle-the-webs-instant-fame.html?pagewanted=all).

Hawk, Thomas. "Zooomr, 17 Year Old Developer Kristopher Tate Building a Photo Sharing Site to Rival Flickr." Thomas Hawk's Digital Connection blog, March 24, 2006. Retrieved November 2011 (http://thomashawk.com/2006/03/zooomr-17-year-old-developer.html).

HubPages.com. "How to Make Money with iPhone Apps." Retrieved October 2011 (http://cool-hubber.hubpages.com/hub/make-money-with-iphone).

Kirpalani, Reshma. "New Jersey Siblings Net $100 Million for myYearbook Sale." *ABC News*, July 22, 2011. Retrieved November 2011 (http://abcnews.go.com/Technology/teens-start-company-sells-100-million/story?id=14127273# .Tshy_WBuHyU).

Kroll, Luisa. "Future 400: Ones to Watch." *Forbes*, September 21, 2011. Retrieved November 15, 2011 (http://www.forbes.com/ sites/luisakroll/2011/09/21/future-400-ones-to-watch).

Lindberg, Oliver. "Kristopher Tate." *.net*, December 18, 2006. Retrieved November 2011 (http://www.netmagazine.com/ interviews/in-depth/kristopher-tate).

Moran, Gwen, and Sue Johnson. *The Complete Idiot's Guide to Business Plans*. 2nd ed. New York, NY: Alpha Books, 2010.

O'Neill, Megan. "Kid Entrepreneur Catherine Cook on Building a Company at Age 15." SocialTimes.com, August 16, 2011. Retrieved November 2011 (http://socialtimes.com/ catherine-cook_b74308).

Scheidies, Nick, and Nick Tart. "Catherine Cook Interview: myYearbook at $20 Million at 20." JuniorBiz.com, June 26, 2010. Retrieved November 2011 (http://juniorbiz.com/ catherine-cook-interview).

Shontell, Alyson. "Siblings Sell 6-Year-Old Startup for $100 Million." MSNBC.com, July 21, 2011. Retrieved November 2011 (http://www.msnbc.msn.com/id/43841557/ns/ business-small_business/t/siblings-sell--year-old-startup-million/#.TsMrxmBuHyV).

Stelter, Brian. "YouTube Videos Pull in Real Money." *New York Times*, December 10, 2008. Retrieved November 2011 (http://www.nytimes.com/2008/12/11/business/media/ 11youtube.html).

Viswanathan, Priya. "Can Android Really Compete with the Apple App Store?" About.com. Retrieved November 2011 (http:// mobiledevices.about.com/od/mobileappbasics/tp/Can-Android-Really-Compete-With-The-Apple-App-Stores.htm).

Wooldridge, Dave, and Michael Schneider. *The Business of iPhone and iPad App Development: Making and Marketing Apps That Succeed*. New York, NY: Apress, 2010.

INDEX

A

Android apps, 29–30
Apple, 10, 28, 29, 35, 38, 48, 50
application content providers (ACPs), 48–50
apps, 21–23, 28, 50
  development platforms, 29–30

B

blogs, 19–21
business plan, writing a, 37–43
  components of, 39–40
  reasons for, 40–43
  templates and software, 41
business structures, 45–47

C

competition, researching, 30–32
concept, developing a, 7–16
Cook, Catherine, 12, 15, 17, 27, 33, 47, 54
Cook, David, 12, 17, 27, 47
corporation, beginning a, 45, 46–47
customers, finding ideal, 26–30

D

developing an idea, 13–15
digitization, defined, 4
domain name registration, 49

E

e-books, and making money, 22–23

F

Facebook, 4, 10, 11, 17, 26–28, 34, 37, 46
filling a need, 10–12, 13–14, 17, 21

H

Hastings, Reed, 15, 30
hidden costs, 33
Hodges, Freddie Ann, 10, 23

I

intellectual property rights, 45, 52–54
interests, identifying your, 7–10

ABOUT THE AUTHOR

Barbara Gottfried Hollander has authored several economics and business books, including *Money Matters: An Introduction to Economics*, *Managing Money*, *Raising Money,* and *Paying for College: Practical, Creative Strategies.* She is an economic content developer and specialized project manager for online education companies. Hollander has also spoken at the Council for Economic Education on the role of technology in the classroom and enjoys managing her own Web site, http://www .awritetolearn.com. She received a B.A. in economics from the University of Michigan and an M.A. in economics from New York University.

PHOTO CREDITS

Cover, pp. 1, 3, 4–5 (numbers, laptops) © iStockphoto.com/ loops7; cover, p. 1 (hand, sphere) © iStockphoto.com/Antonis Papantoniou; pp. 4, 5 (inset images) Cathal Mcnaughton/Reuter/ Landov; pp. 5 (bottom), 7, 17, 26, 37, 45 © iStockphoto.com/ Dennis Glorie; p. 8 Chicago Tribune/Contributor/McClatchy-Tribune; p. 9 Daily Mail/South West News Service Ltd & Masons News; p. 13 Andrew Miller/Newhouse News Service /Landov; p.14 Justin Sullivan/Getty Images; p. 18 Karen Moskowitz/Taxi; p. 20 © AP Images; p. 24 Photo by Ronnie Baker/Plano Star Courier; p. 25 William Andrew/Photographer's Choice: p. 27 Peter DaSilva for the New York Times/Redux; p. 31 BananaStock/ Thinkstock; p. 34 Rashaun Rucker/MCT/Landov; p. 38 iStockphoto/ Thinkstock; p. 43 Andreas Pollok/Taxi; p. 46 © Imago/ZUMA Press; p. 51 © Iain Masterton/age footstock/SuperStock; interior background image (glitter) © iStockphoto.com/Tobias Helbig; remaining interior background image © iStockphoto.com/ Alexander Putyata.

Designer: Brian Garvey; Editor: Andrea Sclarow Paskoff; Photo Researcher: Amy Feinberg